A Drifting Boat

A Drifting Boat

An Anthology of Chinese Zen Poetry

Edited by
Jerome P. Seaton & Dennis Maloney

Translated by
Tony Barnstone, Richard B. Clark, James M. Cryer,
Sam Hamill, Paul Hansen, Chris Laughrun, Joseph Lisowski,
Chou Ping, James H. Sanford, Jerome P. Seaton, Arthur Tobias,
and Jan W. Walls

WHITE PINE PRESS ✌ FREDONIA, NY

Acknowledgements:
All poems translated by Sam Hamill from *Midnight Flute*, Shambala. Copyright 1994 by
Sam Hamill and reprinted by permission.

All poems of Lin Ho-ching (Lin Pu) from *Lin He-Jing: Recluse-Poet of Orphan Mountain*,
Brooding Heron Press. Copyright 1993 by Paul Hansen and reprinted by permission.

All poems of Hsi Chou, Pao T'an, Wen Chao, Heng Chao, Chien Chang, Wei Feng, Hui
Ch'ung, and Yu Chao from *The Nine Monks, Buddhist Poets of the Northern Sung*,
Brooding Heron Press. Copyright 1988 by Paul Hansen and reprinted by permission.

Several of J. P. Seaton's translations of Yuan Mei have appeared in *Cenizas, Negative
Capability, The Literary Review,* and *Shantih*. Poems of Ching An appeared in *Carbuncle
4*.

Several poems by Sam Hamill, Paul Hansen, and Joseph Lisowski were previously pub-
lished in *The Literary Review*.

All poems of Shih-te and Han-shan from *The View From Cold Mountain*, White Pine
Press. © 1982 by J. P. Seaton, James Sanford, and Arthur Tobias and reprinted by per-
mission.

The Hsinh hsin ming from *Hsin hsin ming*, White Pine Press. Copyright 1984 by
Richard Clark and reprinted by permission..

Publication of this book was made possible, in part,
by grants from the New York State Council on the Arts
and the National Endowment for the Arts.

Book design by Elaine LaMattina

Manufactured in the United States of America.

Published by
White Pine Press
10 Village Square, Fredonia, New York 14063

First printing, 1994

9 8 7 6 5 4 3 2

CONTENTS

Sung

Yuan

Ming

Ch'ing & Republican Era

A DRIFTING BOAT

INTRODUCTION

Scholar translators of holy Sanskrit texts, ragged mountain wild-men, nuns and monks, retired civil servants, scholar-officials of the Emperor of China, residents of humble mountain monasteries, Buddhist prelates whose prestige and moral force often made them rivals in secular power to those officials themselves: poets of every century from the sixth to the twentieth are to be found here, clarifying in bright and vibrant poetic lines the transmission of a single ideal. At the same time they demonstrate clearly the multiplicity of manners, the diversity of techniques, and the creative freedom of the human spirit that is the truest embodiment of Ch'an, a brand of Buddhist practice that, born in China, evolved to spread and thrive in East Asia for over fifteen hundred years. A lively and often humorous Way to, and from, spiritual salvation, and a Way of living peacefully and forcefully in the everyday world, better known in the West by its Japanese pronunciation as Zen, it remains full of life in the twentieth century West, continuing to grow and change, and boding well to become as important a feature of the world culture of the tomorrows of the twenty-first century as it has been of a thousand years of Asian yesterdays.

The poetry in this anthology is presented in as close to chronological order as modern scholarship allows. Thus it may offer a little insight into the nature of the evolution of the Ch'an sect, originally a sect fairly narrowly devoted to the path of enlightenment through deep mind meditation, into that living entity that Zen is today. The spiritual passion that supports myriad pathways, both monastic and lay, in the present world, can already be seen in the earliest poetry. The expansion of the Ch'an vision begins in the T'ang Dynasty, maybe not just coincidentally also known as both the Golden Age of Ch'an and the Golden Age of Chinese poetry. It can be seen in works as various as the rough colloquial harangues of the legendary mountain monk Han Shan and the refined meditations of the T'ang scholar-official and renowned painter-poet Wang Wei. Between them these two, with the help of the great monk-poets Chiao-jan, Ling-yi, Kuan Hsiu, and the nine monks of the Sung, and of lay poets like Li Po, Po Chu-yi, Lin Ho-ching and Su Shih, began the confluence of the religious verse of early Ch'an into the great stream with traditional Chinese poetry. There, in addition to deepening the stream bed, this great coming together invigorated Ch'an itself, permitting its interaction with the almost incredible communicative power of the Chinese written language and its great ensemble of poetic techniques and devices. The Ch'an, a school that had learned from Taoism a healthy distrust for words, found a new source of power in the classic poetic language, precisely because that language had been formed on the principle of " no ideas but in things. "

The coexistence from T'ang on of both a monastic and a lay tradition of Ch'an poetry served to keep both sets of poets (often friends) on their toes, stretching to match and to complement each other's accomplishments. The rough shock-poetry of Han Shan and Shih Te, a poetry that mocks pretension and hypocrisy, that slaps the face of the lazy meditator or the foolish follower of convention, runs side by side for a thousand years with an ever developing lay tradition that emphasizes attention and tranquility, self-knowledge and compassionate action in the world. Both remind us of the beauty and the evanescence of life in the world. They remind us also of the ultimate triviality of most of what drags so many humans into the pit of suffering. Both admit and accept weakness while they quietly suggest the possibility of a spiritual strength that awaits only the inward turning eye.

Living Buddhism today includes institutions that differ very little in constitution and function from the sects and churches of the other great spiritual and religious traditions of the modern world. In Zen, Buddhism also possesses an ecumenical school that is not a school, a community of monastic and lay participants in an eclectic and even an experimental practice that remains open to influences from outside its recognized boundaries. This group, one that includes an increasing number of Western poets and artists, follows the oldest pathways of Ch'an, making its goal as much the exploration of the *means* of salvation as it is the liberation of all sentient beings. The exploration of means is after all a means itself.

Though Zen has long been identified in the West with its historically most persistent and peculiar traits, particularly with sitting meditation, (*tso ch'an* or *zazen*) and the koan method, it has in fact been precisely its liveliness, its zest for life, its eclecticism, its spiritual utilitarianism that has always marked Zen as Zen from its earliest manifestation in China. Though it is strongly influenced by the no nonsense naturalism of Chinese Taoism, Ch'an is quintescentially

Mahayana in its concern for salvation. It is the Buddha's big cart, big enough to haul every single sentient being off to that release from suffering called nirvana. In its most native form, Zen shows little drive for bigger temples, little drive for stricter doctrinal lines or "greater" institutional organization: the edifice complex that plagues Christianity is replaced in Ch'an with a good humored, freespirited drive to find more Ways to load on pilgrims of the Way, to find more places for sentient beings to "sit," or to stand or lie down if they must, on the Way to release from illusion. Finally, maybe, it is just this free spirit, this humane consciousness alive in the world that is the true embodiment, the emblem, the being, the making, of Zen.

If Ch'an is, as many claim, not a religion – because it has few institutional and doctrinal structures and strictures – it may not be wrong to say that poetry, in China and in Japan, has been the re-ligion, the binder together, of Ch'an. It is the poetry, with its shared goal of communication of the Way, that ties the monastic community to the lay community, that ties the so many pasts to so many new presents, striving to make a sangha of the whole of human culture in the world.

The poetry in this anthology is the poetry of humans, not divine beings or even of divines. A few of the poets are known to history as Zen Masters, all are clearly seekers of release for themselves and for others. For all them the poems are, as maybe poems should always be, purified expressions of a consciousness that any, having seen, will be led toward. It appears, nonetheless – and the paradox is a hallmark of Zen – also very much a poetry of the human condition, a poetry by and for everyone. There is sorrow as well as joy. There is desire as well as acceptance.

The purity, a purity beyond the reach of pride, of the religious insight of the monk-translator Hui Yuan and the nun Miao Yin is stunning. The *Hsin Hsin Ming* (Verses on the Faith-Mind) of Sengtsan, a treatise in verse that was a seminal force in the creation of Ch'an as we know it, shows clearly the role of specifically poetic sensitivity in the creation of the Zen world view. It is also perhaps the closest of the poems presented here to what would be properly called religious poetry in the West. The joy, the sorrow, the laughter and the rough camaraderie for the road that Han Shan and so many of his incarnations show us in the plainest of plain words is, as Gary Snyder has said, as refreshing as a cool drink of water for the dusty traveler. The keen eyes of Chiao Jan and Po Chu-i invite the reader to see. The open heart of Wang An-shih, controversial social reformer of the Sung Dynasty, may challenge the modern democrat to discover the source of compassion. The irony of Yuan Mei shines a clear light through the illusions of self-importance that may block the path to self-knowledge and release. The self-mockery of Ching-an is the emblem of a humility so deep and yet so lightly put that it invites the reader to see and maybe to lightly mock his or her own spiritual pretensions. All these and more are presented in language that never fails to engage and to delight. The American translators responsible for bringing these voices to life again here are briefly introduced at the end of the anthology. If they had not heard the music of Ch'an, individually and together, these poems would still be available only to the Chinese reader.

It is not wrong to say that Ch'an poetry contains no metaphor: it is the song of phenomena. The mountain is the mountain; the river is the river. A rock in Han Shan, a rock in Yuan Mei, is a rock in the world. Bite it at your peril. Sit in its shade when the sun shines hot on the mountain top. Yet, in a properly paradoxial Way, all Zen poetry, each and all Zen poems taken together, become a single metaphor. Nature, remade real (for your convenience the cart takes another shape) in the words of the poem, encompassed in the purified consciousness, is metaphor for our natures, which are not separate. The moon that shines from all waters is one moon. So many bright moons as the clouds clear away: a single light. Set your boat adrift here, in the midst of it.

—J. P. Seaton

PRE-T'ANG
4th to 7th Century

❧ Hui Yung (332-414)

Translating Sutras

We go on unwinding the woof
from the web of their meaning:
words of the Sutras
day by day leap forth.
Head on we've
chased the miracle
of Dharma:
here are no mere scholars.

Moon Sitting

High mountain cascades froth.
This wild temple owns few lamps.
Sit facing the glitter
of the moon: out of season
heart of ice.

JPS

❧ Miao Yin (fl. 376-380)

Wind and Water

a steady wind scours the autumn moon
from a stagnant pool, from the crystal spring
every place pure now. . . just as it is.
why, then, does karma yet coil and bind?

JPS

∾ Hui K'o (4th-5th Century)

No me: Dharmas all
empty.

Death, Life, small
difference.
Heart of mystery's
transformation:
know, and see.

The Truth cries out
where the arrow strikes the target.

JPS

The Absolute

selfless dharmas are all empty
life and death about alike
the transformed heart knows it all at a glance
truth is in the middle of things.

JHS

∾ Seng Ts'an (d. 606)

Verses on the Faith-Mind

The Great Way is not difficult
for those who have no preferences.
When love and hate are both absent
everything becomes clear and undisguised.
Make the smallest distinction, however,
and heaven and earth are set infinitely apart.
If you wish to see the truth
then hold no opinions for or against anything.
To set up what you like against what you dislike
is the disease of the mind.
When the deep meaning of things is not understood
the mind's essential peace is disturbed to no avail.

The Way is perfect like vast space
where nothing is lacking and nothing is in excess.
Indeed, it is due to our choosing to accept or reject
that we do not see the true nature of things.
Live neither in the entanglements of outer things,
nor in inner feelings of emptiness.
Be serene in the oneness of things
and such erroneous views will disappear by themselves.
When you try to stop activity to achieve passivity
your very effort fills you with activity.
As long as you remain in one extreme or the other
you will never know Oneness.

Those who do not live in the single Way
fail in both activity and passivity,
assertion and denial.
To deny the reality of things
is to miss their reality;
to assert the emptiness of things
is to miss their reality.

The more you talk and think about it,
the further astray you wander from the truth.
Stop talking and thinking,
and there is nothing you will not be able to know.
To return to the root is to find the meaning,
but to pursue appearances is to miss the source.
At the moment of inner enlightenment
there is a going beyond appearance and emptiness.
The changes that appear to occur in the empty world
we call real only because of our ignorance.
Do not search for the truth;
only cease to cherish opinions.

Do not remain in the dualistic state;
avoid such pursuits carefully.
If there is even a trace
of this and that, of right and wrong,
the Mind-essence will be lost in confusion.
Although all dualities come from the One,
do not be attached even to this One.
When the mind exists undisturbed in the Way,
nothing in the world can offend,
and when a thing can no longer offend,
it ceases to exist in the old way.

When no discriminating thoughts arise,
the old mind ceases to exist.
When thought objects vanish,
the thinking-subject vanishes,
as when the mind vanishes, objects vanish.
Things are objects because of the subject [mind];
the mind [subject] is such because of things [objects].
Understand the relativity of these two
and the basic reality: the unity of emptiness.
In this Emptiness the two are indistinguishable
and each contains in itself the whole world.
If you do not discriminate between coarse and fine
you will not be tempted to prejudice and opinion.

To live in the Great Way
is neither easy nor difficult,
but those with limited views
are fearful and irresolute:
the faster they hurry, the slower they go,
and clinging [attachment] cannot be limited;
even to be attached to the idea of enlightenment
is to go astray.
Just let things be in their own way,
and there will be neither coming nor going.

Obey the nature of things [your own nature]
and you will walk freely and undisturbed.
When thought is in bondage the truth is hidden,
for everything is murky and unclear,
and the burdensome practice of judging
brings annoyance and weariness.
What benefit can be derived
from distinctions and separations?

If you wish to move in the One Way
do not dislike even the world of senses and ideas.
Indeed, to accept them fully
is identical with true Enlightenment.
The wise man strives to no goals
but the foolish man fetters himself.
There is one Dharma, not many;
distinctions arise
from the clinging needs of the ignorant;
to seek Mind with the [discriminating] mind
is the greatest of all mistakes.

Rest and unrest derive from illusion;
with enlightenment there is no liking and disliking.
All dualities come from ignorant inference.
They are like dreams or flowers in air:
foolish to try to grasp them.
Gain and loss, right and wrong:
such thoughts must finally be abolished at once.

If the eye never sleeps,
all dreams will naturally cease.
If the mind makes no discriminations,
the ten thousand things
are as they are, of single essence.
To understand the mystery of this One-essence
is to be released from all entanglements.
When all things are seen equally
the timeless Self-essence is reached.
No comparisons or analogies are possible
in this causeless, relationless state.

Consider movement stationary
and the stationary in motion,
both movement and rest disappear.
When such dualities cease to exist
Oneness itself cannot exist.
To this ultimate finality
no law or description applies.

For the unified mnd in accord with the Way
all self-centered striving ceases.
Doubts and irresolutions vanish
and life in true faith is possible.
With a single stroke we are freed from bondage;
nothing clings to us and we hold to nothing.
All is empty, clear, self-illuminating
with no exertion of the mind's power.
Here thought, feeling, knowledge, and imagination
are of no value.
In this world of Suchness
there is neither self nor other-than-self.

To come directly into harmony with this reality
just simply say when doubt arises, 'Not two.'
In this 'not two' nothing is separate,
nothing is excluded.
No matter when or where,
enlightenment means entering this truth.

And this truth is beyond extension or
diminution in time or space;
in it a single thought is ten thousand years.

Emptiness here, Emptiness there,
but the infinite universe stands
always before your eyes.
Infinitely large and infinitely small:
no difference, for definitions have vanished
and no boundaries are seen.
So too with Being and non-Being.
Don't waste time in doubts and arguments
that have nothing to do with this.

One thing, all things:
move among and intermingle,
without distinction.
To live in this realization
is to be without anxiety about non-perfection.
To live in this faith is the road to non-duality,
Because the non-dual is one with the trusting mind.

words!
The Way is beyond language
for in it there is

        no yesterday
        no tomorrow
        no today.

RBC

T'ang
618-905

∿ Han Shan (Legendary, c. 730)

Divination showed my place among these bunched cliffs
where faint trails cut off the traces of men and women
what's beyond the yard
white clouds embracing hidden rocks
living here still after how many years
over and over I've seen spring and winter change
get the word to families with bells and cauldrons
empty fame has no value

. . .

Everyone who reads my poems
must protect the purity of their heart's heart
cut down your craving   continue your days modestly
coax the crooked and the bent   then you'll be upright
drive out and chase away your evil karma
return home and follow your true nature
on that day you'll get the Buddhabody
as swiftly as Lu-ling runs

. . .

Looking for a place to settle out
Cold Mountain will do it
fine wind among thick pines
the closer you listen the better the sound
under them a man   his hair turning white
mumbling mumbling Taoist texts
he's been here ten years unable to return
completely forgotten the way by which he came

. . .

My heart is like the autumn moon
perfectly bright in the deep green pool
nothing can compare with it
you tell me   how it can be explained

. . .

Wanting to go to the eastern cliff
setting out now after how many years
yesterday I used the vines to pull myself up
but halfway there wind and mist made the going tough
the narrow path grabbed at my clothes
the moss so slippery I couldn't proceed
so I stopped right here beneath this cinnamon tree
used a cloud as a pillow and went to sleep

. . .

Sitting alone in peace before these cliffs
the full moon is heaven's beacon
the ten thousand things are all reflections
the moon originally has no light
wide open   the spirit of itself is pure
hold fast to the void   realize its subtle mystery
look at the moon like this
this moon that is the heart's pivot

. . .

I like my home being well hidden
a dwelling place cut off from the world's noise and dust
trampling the grass has made three paths
looking up at the clouds makes neighbors in the four directions
there are birds to help with the sound of the singing
but there isn't anyone to ask about the words of the Dharma
today among these withered trees
how many years make one spring

. . .

People ask the way to Cold Mountain
Cold Mountain   the road doesn't go through
by summer the ice still hasn't melted
sunrise is a blur beyond the fog
imitating me   how can you get here
if your heart was like mine
you'd return to the very center

. . .

I live beneath a green cliff
the weeds I don't mow flourish in the yard
new vines hang down all twisted together
old rocks rise up straight in precipitous slopes
monkeys pick the mountain fruit
egrets catch the pond fish
with one or two of the immortals' books
beneath the trees I mumble   reading aloud

. . .

When the year passes   it's exchanged for a year of worries
but when spring arrives   the colors of things are fresh and new
mountain flowers laugh in green water
cliff trees dance in bluegreen mist
the bees and butterflies express their joy
the birds and fish are even more lovable
my desire for a friend to wander with still unsatisfied
I struggled all night but could not sleep

. . .

Your essays are pretty good
your body is big and strong
but birth provides you with a limited body
and death makes you a nameless ghost
it's been like this since antiquity
what good will come of your present striving
if you could come here among the white clouds
I'd teach you the purple mushroom song

. . .

If you're always silent and say nothing
what stories will the younger generation have to tell
if you hide yourself away in the thickest woods
how will your wisdom's light shine through
a bag of bones is not a sturdy vessel
the wind and frost do their work soon enough
plow a stone field with a clay ox
and the harvest day will never come

. . .

In the green creek spring water is clear
at Cold Mountain the moon's corona is white
silence your understanding and the spirit of itself is enlightened
view all things as the Void and this world is even more still

. . .

My resting place is in the deep woods now
but I was born a farmer
growing up simple and honest
speaking plainly without flattery
what nourished me wasn't studying for jade badges of office
but believing that a man of virtue would then get the pearl
how can we be like those floating beauties
wild ducks drifting on the waves as far as the eye can see

. . .

Clouds and mountains all tangled together up to the blue sky
a rough road and deep woods without any travellers
far away the lone moon a bright glistening white
nearby a flock of birds sobbing like children
one old man sitting alone   perched in these green mountains
a small shack   the retired life   letting my hair grow white
pleased with the years gone by   happy with today
mindless this life is like water flowing east

. . .

In my house there is a cave
in the cave there's nothing at all
pure emptiness   really wonderful
glorious and splendid   bright as the sun

vegetarian fare nourishes this old body
cotton and hides cover this illusory form
let a thousand saints appear before me
I have the Dharmakaya for my very own

. . .

Despite the obstacles I pursued the great monk
the misty mountains a million layers high
he pointed to the road back home
one round moon   lantern of the sky

. . .

Ahead   the green creek sparkles as it flows
toward the cliff   a huge rock with a good edge for sitting
my heart is like a lone cloud   with nothing to depend on
so far away from the world's affairs.
                    what need is there to search for anything

. . .

When this generation sees Han-shan
they all say I'm a crazy man
unworthy of a second look
this body wrapped only in cotton and hides
they don't understand what I say
I don't speak their kind of jabber
I want to tell all of you passing by
you can come up and face Cold Mountain

. . .

Me   I'm happy with the everyday way
like the mist and vines in these rockstrewn ravines
this wilderness is so free and vast
my old friends   the white clouds   drift idly off
there is a road   but it doesn't reach the world
mindless   who can be disturbed by thoughts
at night I sit alone on a stone bed
while the round moon climbs the face of Cold Mountain

                . . .

Amidst a thousand clouds and ten thousand streams
there lives one ex-scholar   me
by day wandering these green mountains
at night coming home to sleep beneath a cliff
suddenly spring and fall have already passed by
and no dust has piled up to disturb this stillness
such happiness   what do I depend on
here it's as tranquil as autumn river water

                . . .

I see people chanting a sutra
who depend on its words for their ability to speak
their mouths move but their hearts do not
their hearts and mouths oppose each other
yet the heart's true nature is without conflict
so don't get all tangled up in the words
learn to know your own bodily self
don't look for something else to take its place
then you'll become the boss of your mouth
knowing full well there's no inside or out

AT

~ Shih Te (Legendary, c. 730)

Since I came to this T'ien T'ai temple
how many Winters and Springs have passed
the mountains and the waters are unchanged
the man's grown older
how many other men will watch those mountains stand

. . .

see the moon's bright blaze of light
a shining lamp, above the world
full glistening and hanging in vast void
that brilliant jewel, its brightness, through the mist

some people say it waxes, wanes
their's may but mine remains
as steady as the Mani Pearl
this light knows neither day or night

. . .

sermons there are, must be a million
too many to read in a hurry
if you want a friend just come to T'ien T'ai mountain
sit deep among the crags
we'll talk about the Principles
and chat about dark Mysteries
if you don't come to my mountain
your view will be blocked
by the others

. . .

if you want to catch a rat
you don't need a fancy cat
it you want to learn the Principles
don't study fine bound books
the True Pearl's in a hemp sack
the Buddha nature rests in huts
many grasp the sack
but few open it.

　　　.　.　.

I laugh at myself, old man, with no strength left
inclined to piney peaks, in love with lonely paths
oh well, I've wandered down the years to now
free in the flow; and floated home the same
　　　　　a drifting boat.

　　　.　.　.

not going, not coming
rooted, deep and still
not reaching out, not reaching in
just resting, at the center
a single jewel, the flawless crystal drop
in the blaze of its brilliance
the way beyond

　　　.　.　.

a long way off, I see men in the dirt
enjoying whatever it is that they find in the dirt
when I look at them there in the dirt
my heart wells full of sadness

why sympathize with men like these?
I can remember the taste of that dirt.

. . .

cloudy mountains, fold on fold,
            how many thousands of them?
shady valley road runs deep, all trace of man is gone
green torrents, pure clear flow, no place more full of beauty
and time, and time, birds sing
            my own heart's harmony.

. . .

if you want to be happy
there's no other way than the hermit's
flowers in the grove, endless brocade
every single season's colors new
just sit beside the chasm
turn your head, as the moon rolls by
yet though I ought to be at joyous ease
I can't stop thinking of the others.

. . .

far, far, the mountain path is steep
thousands of feet up, the pass is dangerous and narrow
on the stone bridge the moss and lichen green
from time to time, a sliver of cloud flying
cascades hang like skeins of silk
image of the moon from the deep pool shining
once more to the top of Flowering Peak

there waiting, still
the coming of the solitary crane

. . .

Idle, I visited the high monks
green mountain, white clouds
next door crying children
on the other side a boisterous crowd
the Five-Peaks touch the Milky Way
the cobalt sky is clear as water
true, they pointed my way home
pool of lamplight beneath the moon.

JHS, JPS

~ P'ei Ti & Wang Wei (700-761)

Meng Wall Cove

Below the ancient city's wall lies
My thatched hut. In time I'll climb
Those old walls in disrepair
Where others now merely pass by.

By this new home near the old city wall
Ancient trees fringe weeping willows.
Here anyone can begin again, but first
The heart must be empty of sorrow.

Hua-tzu Hill

A dappled sunset, and the pine wind rises.
Turning to home, I notice the grass thin, spare,
Above, clouds patch like footprints
The dazzling mountain, dampening our robes.

Birds ride the currents endlessly
Against the autumn-splashed mountain.
Up and down Hua-tzu Hill they soar —
What sadness my heart bears!

Deer Park

Morning and night I see cold mountain
Then to be alone, an unattended guest.
Not knowing the way of pine groves,
I only follow the tracks of deer and doe.

On the empty mountain no one is seen.
There's only the sound of voices.
Light enters dazzling the deep grove
And again the moss is brilliant green.

Magnolia Enclosure

Bright green mists at sunset,
Birds chirp wildly against the swift stream.
Its green current runs deep
Then dark a long, long time.

Autumn mountains compress the bursting light.
Flying birds press close to one another.
Bright clouds, blue flashing bright –
The evening mist stops nowhere.

Lakeside Pavilion

From the window a rippling of waves,
The solitary moon drifts back and forth.
From the gorge shoot gibbons' cries.
The wind carries them to where I sit.

A light barge for the welcome guests
Comes from far up the lake.
Before the windows, they toast with wine.
Everywhere hibiscus begin to open.

South Hillock

A lone boat moors leeward.
At South Hillock, lake waters lap the bank.
The sun sets behind Mount Yen Tzu.
Clear ripples against the immense watery main.

A light boat sails to South Hillock.
From North Hillock, there's a panic of water.
At shore, a man looks toward home
So distant, so far, he can hardly remember.

Lake Yi

Such immense emptiness, the lake's without limit.
Dazzling blue water and sky alike.
Anchor the boat with one long whistle.
From every direction, good winds blow.

Flute music sounds from beyond the shore.
Sunset accompanies my honored guest.
On the lake, I turn my head
To green mountains, whitle curling clouds.

Rill of the House of Luans

The river's voice with whispers to the distant shore
Along a path to South Ferry
Ducks floating, sea gulls flying across.
Time and again they drift close to men.

A gust suddenly rises in the autumn rain.
The shallow stream breaks against the rocks.
Waves ripple, dashing into each other.
A white heron shrieks then dives.

White Rock Rapids

Standing on the rocks, gazing at the water below,
Watching the play of ripples is endless pleasure.
At sunset, it's cold on the river.
Clouds drift by, ordinary, without color.

White Rock Rapids are clear but shallow.
Green rushes bunch rustling nearby.
Houses stretch east and west of the water.
Women wash gauze under a bright moon.

North Hillock

On North Hillock of South Mountain
A thatched cottage overlooks Lake Yi.
Everyone leaves to gather firewood.
A flat boat drifts from the rushes.

At North Hillock, north of the lake,
Brilliant trees are reflected; a red railing
Winds along the south river's edge
Bright like fire against the green grove.

Bamboo Grove

I come humbly to the bamboo grove
Each day hoping to embrace the Way.
Going and coming, there are only mountain birds.
In the profound dark, there is no one.

Alone I sit within the dark bamboo
Strumming my lute, whistling along
In the deep grove no one knows
The bright moon, how we shine together.

Hsin-yi Village

On a green knoll covered with spring grass,
The princely lord loiters alone.
Among the Hsin-yi flowers
The red hibiscus vibrate.

From the end of its branch, the hibiscus flowers.
From the mountain's depth, red stems push.
Along a mountain stream, a vacant cabin stands
Amidst the hibiscus endless bloom and fall.

Lacquer-Tree Garden

Love of leisure is as natural as morning sun.
I accept the fruits born of my past.
Today, I amble through the lacquer-tree garden
And return to the joy Chuang Tzu felt.

The ancient sage was no proud official.
He avoided the warp and weave of the world
And held only a trifling position, casually regarded,
Like an old woman sauntering among twigs of trees.

JL

∿ Li Po (701-762)

Zazen on the Mountain

The birds have vanished down the sky.
Now the last cloud drains away.

We sit together, the mountain and me,
until only the mountain remains.

Old Dust

We live our lives as wanderers
until, dead, we finally come home.

One quick trip between heaven and earth,
then the dust of ten thousand generations.

The Moon-Rabbit mixes elixirs for nothing.
The Tree of Long Life is kindling.

Dead, our white bones lie silent
when pine trees lean toward spring.

Remembering, I sigh; looking ahead, I sigh once more:
This life is mist. What fame? What glory?

I Make My Home in the Mountains

You ask why I live
alone in the mountain forest,

and I smile and am silent
until even my soul grows quiet:

it lives in the other world,
one that no one owns.

The peach trees blossom.
The water continues to flow.

SH

~ Ling Yi (d. 762)

Riverbank Epiphany

these evenings the hills are green again
the streams in the woods clear again.
I know nothing about taming oxen
or of deep grottos, endlessly wide.

above a rustic bank, mists begin to gather
calm waters, but no moon above
a solitary boat might lose its way.
just listen to the rushing autumn springs.

Keepsake for the Old Man of Chung-chou

a lifetime of no place to rest
thousands of miles, overwhelmed and alone
lost my way among the sweet grasses
tear-streaked after the flow of spring currents.

how many seasons of innkeeper's meals?
how many nights in brookside hamlets?
I long for the pains lovers know;
in the empty hills gibbons sing down a setting sun.

JHS

Letter to a wandering husband: Go Home.

Tear drop frozen
to its heart
the letter will come

to tell you of the woman waiting
in the willow garden.

Feelings, knowing
they're hard to guard as
chastity, alone.

Again, here, and there the sun's
first rays of Spring.

JPS

~ Tu Fu (712-770)

Visiting the Monastery at Lung-men

I explored the grounds with monks this evening,
and now the night has passed.

Heavy silence rises all around us
while late moonlight spills through the forest.

The mountain rises almost into heaven.
Sleeping in the clouds is cold.

A single stroke of the early prayer-bell awakens one,
but does it also waken the soul?

SH

∾ Chiao Jan (730?-799?)

Inscribed on the Wall of the Hut by the Lake

If you want to be a mountain dweller . . .
no need to trek to India to find one.
I've got a thousand peaks
to pick from, right here in the lake.
Fragrant grasses, white clouds,
to hold me here.
What holds you there,
world-dweller?

To be Shown to the Monks at a Certain Temple

Not yet to the shore of non-doing,
it's silly to be sad you're not moored yet. . .
Eastmount's white clouds say
to keep on moving, even
it it's evening, even if it's Fall.

At Gusu

The ancient terrace now invisible:
Autumn grasses wither, there
where once the King of Wu stood
proud and strong. A thousand
years of moonlight on the grass:
how many times did he gaze down upon it?
Now the moon will rise again, but he
will not. A world of men have
gazed, will gaze, upon great
Gusu Mountain. Here dwells a placid spirit.
Deer herd to blur men's footprints.
Here too Hsi-tzu's fair simplicity, seductive
lips brought an Empire crashing down:
now, that all is change is clear:
at Cold Peak, a little heap of dirt.

Metaphor

My Tao: at the root, there's no me...
yet I don't despise worldly men.
Just now I've been into the city...
so I know I really mean that.

Human Life

Human life, a hundred years?
                    I've passed a half of them.
The talents I was born with
                    can't be changed.
I angled for big turtles in the Eastern Sea
                    but the turtles wouldn't bite.
I sat with the stones at South Mountain
                    till they were way past ripe.

Goodbyes

I've heard that even "men of feeling"
            hate the feeling of parting.
Frosty sky drips a chill
                    on the cold city wall.
The long night spreads
                    like water overflowing.
There's the sound of the watch-horn, too.
The Zen man's heart is empty, yes,
                    of all but this.

Cold Night, I Heard the Sounding of the Watch, and Wrote This Letter to a Friend

Leaning on my pillow,
I heard the watch-drum, cold.
Cold that changes, cold that stays.
One night, a thousand, ten thousand soundings.
How many did you hear there?

Gazing at T'ien-chu and Ling-yin Temples

On the mountain, East and West, a temple . . .
In the river, sunrise and sunset, the flow.
A heart for home, but no way to get there . . .
A road through the pines
and the blue-green mist.

Sending Off a Friend
Amidst the Cries of Gibbons

You go ten thousand miles
beyond those Western Mountains . . .
Three gibbons' cries,
a chasm full of moonlight . . .
How long's this road been here?
How many travelers
have wet their sleeves beside it?
A broken wall divides the drooping shadows.
Rushing rapids sing a bitter song.
In the cold, after we part,
it will be all the more wounding to hear.

Gazing at the Moon from South Tower

Moon tonight, and everyone's moon-gazing,
but I'm alone, and in love with this tower.
Threads of cloud are shattered in the stream:
trailing willow is the picture of late Fall.
As it brightens, you can see a thousand peaks.
Far off, the veins of ridges flow.
Mountain passes . . .
will I ever climb again?
I stand alone,
and let the border sadness rise.

JPS

∾ Chang Chi (768-830)

Lament

We carved our names in a courtyard near the river
when you were youngest of all our guests.

But you will never see bright spring again,
nor the beautiful apricot blossoms

that flutter silently past
the open temple door.

SH

∿ Han Yu (768-824)

Mountain Rocks

Ragged mountain rocks efface the path.
Twilight comes to the temple and bats hover.
Outside the hall I sit on steps and gaze at torrential new rain.
Banana leaves are wide, the cape jasmine is fat.
A monk tells me the ancient Buddhist frescos are good
and holds a torch to show me, but I can barely see.
I lie quiet in night so deep even insects are silent.
From behind a rise the clear moon enters my door.
In the dawn I am alone and lose myself,
wandering up and down in mountain mist.
Then colors dazzle me: mountain red, green stream,
and a pine so big, ten people linking hands can't encircle it.
Bare feet on slick rock as I wade upstream.
Water sounds shhhh, shhhh. Wind inflates my shirt.
A life like this is the best.
Why put your teeth on the bit and let people rein you in?
O friends, my party of gentlemen,
how can we grow old without returning here?

TB & CP

~ Liu Tsung-Yuan (773-819)

River Snow

A thousand mountains. Flying birds vanish.
Ten thousand paths. Human traces erased.
One boat, bamboo hat, bark cape – an old man.
Alone with his hook. Cold river. Snow.

TB & CP

~ Wu Pen (Chia Tao, 779-841)

After Finishing a Poem

Those two lines cost me three years:
I chant them once, and get two more, of tears.
Friend, if you don't like them . . .
I'll go home, and lie down,
in the ancient mountain autumn.

Overnight at a Mountain Temple

Flock of peaks hunched up
and colored cold. Path forks
here, toward the temple.
A falling star flares behind bare trees,
and the moon breasts the current of the clouds.
To the very top, few men come;
one tall pine won't hold a flock of cranes.
One monk here, at eighty,
has never heard tell
of the "world" down below.

Quatrain

At the bottom of the ocean: moon,
bright moon, round as the wheel
of the sky. Just get a single hand
full of this glory . . .
and you could buy a thousand miles of Spring.

JPS

A Letter Sent

The family's living up Brocade Creek,
while I've struggled off to this distant sea.
Of ten letters sent, maybe one gets through,
and when it does it says
another year's gone by.

Parting with the Monk Ho-lan

Wild monk, come to make a parting
with me. We sit a while on the sand
beside the welling source . . .
A far way you'll go
on an empty alms bowl,
deep among mountains,
treading fallen flowers.
Masterless Ch'an, our
own understanding . . .
When you've got it, there's no place
for it but a poem. This parting's nothing
fated: orphan clouds just never settle down.

The Swordsman

Ten long years I've honed this sword:
frost white blade as yet untried.
Today, like any other gentleman,
it's looking for injustice.

Extempore

Midnight, heart
                    startled,
I rise,
to take the path to Long Cascade:
grove's trees swallowed in white dew, a dipper
of stars, in the clear dark sky.

JPS

~ Po Chu-i (772-846)

Staying at Bamboo Lodge

an evening sitting under
     the eaves of the pines
at night sleeping
     in Bamboo Lodge
the sky so clear you'd say
     it was drugs
meditation so deep, thought
     I'd gone home to the hills
          but Clever can't beat
          Stupid
          and Quick won't match
          Quiet
Untoiling-ness!
     (you just can't pave the Way)
that's it!
     the Gate of Mystery!

Autumn's Cold

here's my snowy crown
        time's tinted decrepitude
there's the frost in the courtyard
        autumn's glittery breath
now I'm sick and just watching my wife
        pick cure-alls
then I'm frozen waiting for the maid
        to comb my hair
without the body
        what use fame?
worldly things
        I've put aside
tranquilly
        I delve my heart
determined now
        to learn from Empty Boats!

Above the Pond

mountain monks
        over their chess game sit
over a board where
        bamboo shadows plainly show
and though through sunset's glare
        no bamboo can be seen
sometimes I hear a sound
        like chess men falling

Pondside

I

I've finished the pavillion
　　　　on the pond's west bank
cleared out the trees
　　　　across to the east
and this
　　　　no one understands. . .
but I just wanted a place
　　　　to wait on the moon

II

knife in hand I
　　　　chop the thick bamboo
for the less the bamboo
　　　　the more the wind
and this
　　　　no one comprehends. . .
but all I want is
　　　　to make waves on the pond

May: The Pond's Full

May and the pond's full of water
        wandering turtles, dancing fish
I love it so much I've
        started a house there
despite the tribal disparities of men and fish
        for what makes both happy, makes both one
fact is, I've become a disciple and
        transcendentally together we pass the days
they, given up on the Vast Oceans
        have taken charge of cattails and the duckweed
I, quit from the Blue Sky Bureaucracy
        am pleased to crawl amongst the bean rows
but though we're of a kind
        we're not River Dragon types
and when cloud and rain come
        it's just us pond critters here!

Crane

though everyone possesses
        some skill
all creatures at heart
        lack constancy
some say
        you're a dancer. . .
best stick
        to standing on fences

Lute

my lute set aside
        on the little table
lazily I meditate
        on cherishing feelings
the reason I don't bother
        to strum and pluck?
there's a breeze over the strings
        and it plays itself

JMC

➷ T'ung-shan Liang Chieh (807-869)

Green Mountains father white clouds:
white clouds are the children of mountains.
White clouds hang around all day.
Mostly the mountain doesn't mind.

JPS

∾ Hsueh-feng Yi Ts'un (821-906)

Ten thousand miles without one
blade of grass. Far, far, colors
lost in smoke and haze. Kalpas
so long . . . What's the use
of shaving your head and
leaving home?

JPS

∾ Shen Ying (fl. 860-874)

Old Monk

Sun shines back
from West Mount's snows:

old monk's gate's not open yet.

Water pitcher's frozen
to the pillar's plinth:
banked night fire almost
lost in the stove's ashes.

His boy is sick,
gone home.
Cold fawn nuzzles
at his door.

Temple bell, and knowing
grows nearer: bird from the branch
will drop in to share
of the mendicant's meal.

JPS

∾ Chih Liang (c. 850)

Singing of Cloud Mountain

I.

People may talk about a ladder to heaven.
Ten million rungs, and each an illusion . . .
Better the old man
sitting, on the cliff
Breeze clear, moon bright,
and his heart,
the same.

II.

Cloud Mountain's top
and the white clouds, level.
Climb to the top and then you'll know
just how low the world is.
Strange herbs, rare
blossoms people wouldn't recognize,
and a spring that runs down
in nine separate streams.

JPS

～ Liang Yi (c. 850)

Answering Lu Ye

I heard wind and waterfall
in a dream: I have nothing
else to send you.
The wheel outside the door is just the moon.
Those objects hanging from the eaves,
just Autumn clouds.

JPS

～ Hsiu Mu (Late 9th Century)

Longing for an Old Garden

I remember a garden I used to visit;
just thinking about it leaves me heartsick.
I sit alone in the weeds along the bank
as the river flows away into a long spring day.

JHS

∾ Huai Su (Late 9th Century)

Written on Mr. Chang's Painting
of the Drunken Monk

Everybody sends him wine . . .
He's no need to beg or barter.

Trailing his days away
beneath the pines
propped against the winepot

The Master of the Brush
when he seeks True Accomplishment
drinks himself mad
for starters,

and threatens to paint himself
into the picture.

JPS

～ Ching Yun (Late 9th Century)

Painting a Pine

This time I think
I got it: one pine real
as the real.

Think about it:
search in memory, is it
real, or not?

Guess I'll have to go
back up the mountain. . .
South past Stonebridge,
the third one on the right. . .

JPS

∿ Kuan Hsiu (832-912)

Moonlit Night

as I wander aimlessly under a frozen moon
a flute pours its beauty from a nearby tower.
then morning breezes begin to rise and gust –
the river already a carpet of scattered white blossoms.

JHS

Letter to the Wild Monk

Other than the birds,
who loves you?
Lordly peaks, your
neighbors.
White head cold pillowed
on a stone.
Grey robe ragged
but not soiled.
Chestnuts pile up on your path.
Monkeys circle where you sit.
If you ever set up another Zendo,
I swear I'll be the one who sweeps the floors.

Moored on Fall River

Banks like Lake Tung-t'ing, but
the hills too steep.

Boat floats the clear stream, but
the cold climbs in my berth.

White moon rides a high wind,
and I can't sleep.

Among the withered reeds
the fisherman's
a nightmare.

Spending the Night in a Little Village

Hard traveling, and then
a little village, for the night:
a year of plenty, chickens, dogs,
it's raucous as a market town.
Come out to meet the stranger in the dusk:
whole families, laughing, happy:
beneath the moon,
seining up fish from the pool.

To an Old Monk on Mount T'ien T'ai

Living alone where none other dwells,
shrine among the pines where mountain tints encroach,
old man's been ninety years a monk:
heart beyond the clouds a lifetime long.
White hair hangs down, his head's unshaven:
clear black pupils smile deep mysteries.
He can still point to the orphan moon
for me alone, relaxes his discipline, this moment.

Thinking of the Old Mountains Toward the End of Autumn

Used to live north of Square Hut . . .
Nobody knew my name.
Up through the clouds to harvest my grain,
climbing like an ant into the tree to pick the oranges.
Saw a tiger wander by that lonesome village . . .
Anyone could grow white haired
living a life like that.

JPS

ᴂ Tzu Lan (c. 890)

Snow

dense, soundless, falling through azure emptiness
swirling clouds sing and dance in the soft breeze.
as the recluse hums a line in praise of hidden places
vagrant flakes drift in and stain his inkstone black.

JHS

❧ Yun Piao (9th-10th Century)

Cold Food Festival Day

The Day of Cold Food, sadly looking
on the Spring outside the city wall:
no place in the wild fields that doesn't somehow
wound my spirit.
The Broad Plain's already scarred with grave mounds:
now we'll add a few, and half of them
were mourners here, last year.

JPS

ᔋ Chih Hsuan (fl. 874-889)

In Praise of Flowers

blossoms opened and turned the forest red
then fell and left ten-thousand empty branches
only one remnant flower lingers on
crimson sun, hanging in the wind.

JHS

❧ Yin Luan (9th-10th Century)

Lute

its seven strings call forth strange, deep thoughts
swirling waters and evergreen winds wait beneath my fingers
I need a listener to draw out these subtle currents

I would teach,

      but who will listen?

Meeting an Old Man

on the road I met an old man
both our heads white as snow.
we walked one mile, then two
taking four rests, then five.

JHS

～ Shu Shan K'uang-jen (9th-10th Century)

My road's beyond blue emptiness . . .
There's no place the white clouds can't go.
Here, there's a trunkless tree:
the wind gives all of its yellow leaves back.

JPS

❧ Hsu Hsuan

Lung-men Village, Autumn

Refusing worldly worries,
I stroll among village strollers.

Pine winds sing, the evening village
smells of grass, autumn in the air.

A lone bird roams down the sky.
Clouds roll across the river.

You want to know my name?
— a hill, a tree. An empty drifting boat.

SH

Sung
960-1278

❧ Lin Ho-ching (965-1026)

Mountain Valley Temple

Just getting
Into the Zen Grove,
I'm still less inclined to leave.
Massed peaks and deep gorges
Circle a lofty cliff.

Tower and terrace
Pierce into the cold
Past cloud and vegetation.
Bell and chime
Rap clearly
Along creeks and rock,
Lifting tea-trays,
A boy takes them to clean.
Leaning on his staff,
The old monk relaxes.

A solitary chamber —
I read inscriptions here,
Nearly make a title out,
Brush the dappled moss.

Self-Portrait at a Little Hermitage

Bamboo and trees
Wind round my hut:
Pure, deep,
hinting at more.

Idle cranes
Prolong their watergazing.
Lazy bees sip flowers.
Hungover,
I can't open a book,
Go hoeing
In spring shade.

And sympathize
With the old-time painters,
Drawing woodcutters
And fishermen.

Monastery on Hsiu-ch'i

Down below
By the district town
Mountain cliffs
Reveal
A monastery gate.

Across the Huai delta
An occasional bell tolling.
One path enters
The root of a cloud.
Bamboos so old
The wind drones through.
Pool so pure,
Its ancient source
Appears.

A lofty monk
Dusts the sutra stand:
Tea and talk
Till dark.

Living as a Recluse on the Lake

Lakewater
Comes into the yard.
Mountains
Wind round my hut.
A recluse
Should avoid the world.

Normally shut,
The unused door's turned blue with moss.
Guests arrive,
Frightening white birds to flight.
Selling herbs,
I almost hate to price them,
Love watering the garden
According to nature.

And how about
India Road
Through the woods,
Still reaching deep autumn
In a distant,
Blue dream?

On the Lake Returning Late

Lying back,
Bulwark for a pillow,
Homebound thoughts so pure
I mistake the view ahead
For Immortals Island.

Through the bridge span
Autumn has tinted trees and water.
Evening just clearing,
Temples lean
Into cloudy peaks.
Avoiding me on sight,

Kingfishers
Make a wet takeoff.
Scent of red lotus
Wafts in welcome.

I gradually near
A vague clearing.
Through the woods
chickens and dogs
Distantly squabble.

Spring Day on West Lake

My talent
Won't compare
With Tu Mu-chih's
But writing poems
Out on the lake
Is worth a try.

In spring mist
A monastery drum
Sounds the forenoon meal.
In evening light
Restaurant flags
Crown buildings and terraces.
Thickly drifting,
Mingled scents
Perfume the cliffs.
In wet flight
Two kingfishers
Brush the ripples.

A good thing
People weave
Grass hats and raincoats,
Board boats,
Become fishermen.

A Recluse on Orphan Mountain
(Written on a Wall)

Until deep into mountain and river
The gibbons and birds are few.
This lifetime I still might move:
Above the creek past India Village.
Log for a bridge,
I'll build a little hut.

PH

❧ Chih Yuan (fl. late 10th century)

Sent to Retired Scholar Lin Ho-ching

Reflecting
In the lake,
Mountain tints fade.
How can dust
From the world oppress?
Far, far,
Color of mist and wave.
Green, green,
Shade of cloud and tree.

Overgrown with moss,
the rocky path's precarious.
Deep past Peach Spring
A dog barks.
There a sage-king
Follows his idle mind.
When flowers bloom
He even toasts them alone.
When they fall,
Chants poetry alone.

In the empty courtyard
Precious grasses grow.
Under dim trees
Immortal birds call.
For three years
I haven't seen you
Humble regret
Fills my empty heart.
Finally
When the Autumn Moon's bright,

I'll ride my inspiration,
Make a casual visit.

PH

～ Hsi Chou (fl. late 10th century)

Theme on the Officials' Rest Pavillion,
Wu-Tang Prefecture

This prefectural pavillion
Is called Officials' Retreat; here
Leisure itself commissions, sir,
The heart.

Roll up the screen
You know a guest has come;
Birds stay the night,
A dangling lamp shows where.
Tea mist strikes a boulder,
Cut off. Go stones echo,
Flower deep.

Since to meet waits the luck
Of a south-bound sail,
I'll seize the autumn,
Mail off
These mumbles.

Sending Off Ssu Tuan to Return East

In distant thoughts
Springs and rock take life:
You are shutting down
Business among people.

Packing clothes
While trees in town
Drop leaves, you seek temples
In the far coastal range:
Sail's reflection
Confuses freezing geese; chant
Of sútras drowns
Dusk tide.

Before
We even plan
Another visit, frosts
Will nip
My hair.

PH

～ Pao T'an (fl. late 10th century)

Old Monk

Down his temples
Tumbles snowy hair.
No talk for visitors.

Patched robe
Hugged tight, sitting
Ends the day. How few springs
Does a floating life
Know? To board a gangway
Evokes dreams of Yüeh;
To grip his staff
Recalls Ch'in rambles.

Midnight,
The frozen halls shut.
A chime sounds:
He hears it
Everywhere.

Written at Candidate Hsu's Villa on the Ti River

The distant
Ferry road blurs;
A traveler's heart
I can't let go.

Half the sky,
Mountains far and near;
Icy day, a river
East and west. Waves
On the slough shrink
Fishing nets; in driven sand
Lines of geese
Dip low.

Frosty wind
Raises deep night,
Missing only
A gibbon's howl.

PH

❧ Wen Chao (fl. late 10th century)

Hidden Garden

Deep in spring
When it rains,
Just a distant bridge
Reaches the village.

Fragrant orchids?
No one's picked them yet;
Fallen flowers? Butterflies
Know first. Thick grass seals
An unused path; open woods
Reveal a low hedge.

Since I left
The hoeing's long-neglected.
I'm old myself,
Hate being away so long.

Sedge-Crown Courtyard

Invisibly trailing,
Sedge clumps and spreads:
Sharp chill, sudden
Rain clears.

Spent autumn
Idles strangers' stroll. Dusk
Jumbles chirping crickets. Straggling
Up mossy steps nearby, sedge-clumps
Level, link bamboo paths
Far-off.

Back and forth
Tracks from hiking sticks
And clawprint of crane
Naturally crisscross.

PH

~ Heng Chao (fl. late 10th century)

Mid-Autumn Moon

Twilight rain
Crosses vast space. River sky
Just grey-green.

Treelines
Miss lingering shadows. Piling water
Retains different light. Everywhere
Hidden insects call. Roosting birds
Startle to sudden flight,

As if the eternal evening
Were utterly impartial
Overlooking me, murmur
A pure passage.

PH

∿ Chien Chang (fl. late 10th century)

Written on Master Heng Chao's Wall

A Zen path
The autumn moss grows over;
Icy windows bear streaks
Of rain.

The true mind
Mysteriously integrates
Itself, but who appreciates
Good poems? Dew chills;
Cricket noises muffle.
A light wind fans
Shadows of foliage.

As if intent,
All day in the window
White clouds.

Sending Off a Monk to Wu-t'ai Mountain

Mount Wu-t'ai
Crosscuts the Milky Way;
Alcedine rock freezes
Toward azure darkness.

Drifted snows don't hold
Defiling heat; tall fir
Block shooting stars. You see
Rock appear out the eaves
When clouds recede, hear
Border bugles blow
In sitting meditation.

The night you arrive
To dwell in Zen,
Rinse your jug alone
In waterfall foam.

PH

～ Wei Feng (fl. late 10th century)

Sent to Academician Ch'en
at the Institute for the Illumination of Literature

Deep autumn
Beyond the wilds,
This stranger climbs a terrace
Facing the capitol.

My long-distance letter
Wasn't sealed and sent
When, by wing of wild geese,
Another arrived from you.
Frozen earth stunts
Border trees; the pure heavens
Break up sickly clouds.

Over limitless distance
Your heart watches; at ease
In the South Palace, your letter
Brilliant as brocade.

Grieving for Zen Master Chien Chang

A frosty bell
Anxiously overrides the waterclock;
Grieving together,
Dense sorrow dawns.

Guests from the coast
Exchange his enlightened poems;
Monks from these woods
Describe his bearing while ill.
The cleansing spring
Floats a fallen leaf;
On rock concentrations
Chirping crickets assemble.

Turning, I view
Cloud Gate Mountain:
Dwindling Sun descends
The distant peak.

PH

∾ Hui Ch'ung (fl. late 10th century)

Visiting Yang Yun-shih's Villa on the Huai River

The place is close,
We got there in a hurry
And, hand in hand, turned
Toward the wilderness pavillion.

The river dividing
Breaks the hill's contour;
Spring's coming quickgreens
Burned-over fields.
We looked around so long,
The fishermen reeled in their lines,
Talked so much, the cranes
All took off.

Don't fret it's late
For the walk back;
A bright Moon's climbing
Islands ahead.

PH

∿ Yu Chao (late 10th century)

Offered to Gentlemen-in-Attendance Ch'ien
at the Library of Assembled Sages

Spiritual cultivation
Implies relinquishing office;
Your pure name crowns
The Library of Assembled Sages.

Excellently traveled
In the prefecture of letters,
You laugh and chat, front-ranked
On the carriage of imperial service.
Court morning you drop
Crane-feather Taoist robes,
Though in the sleeping place
Maps of mountains hang.

When this river monk
Is free for a solitary call,
Then we'll talk
Of woods,
Of springs.

Staying at the Residence of Academician Ting
Chu Yen and Hsi Chou Didn't Arrive

At our private meeting
You didn't appear. Forlorn, I look
Toward your noble feelings.

I've sat so long
The poetic source is silent,
Talked so much,
The rippling well stilled. Touching
Icy trees, the Moon
Goes out. Crickets chirp
Ignoring the cold lamp.

Empty, I listen.
A temple
West of the canal,
The night bell
Rings out
Strict purity.

PH

～ Wei Ye (d. 1019)

On an Autumn Night I Write My Feelings Out

Nearly midnight
I sit in the woods alone;
Leaves fall everywhere
Brush my worn robe.

Lunar shadows slowly shift;
Cricket rythms tense.
Dew glimmers surface;
Cranes sound aloft.
The Four Seasons rush old age;
Autumn especially affects me.
Ten-thousand aims
Twist the mind
Night really wears.

Alone,
I trust
The pure wind
Knows what I think:
Mostly sighing
In the courtyard bamboo,
It helps the melancholy.

Writing the Events of a Winter Day

This year the first month,
The days aren't warm;
When cold hits the village
What do people do?

Idly
Hearing a woodpecker —
Is a monk at the door
Begging?
Crossed with snow,
The pine tint deepens;
Carrying ice,
A creek crashes harsh.

I chant a poem
And turn to silent sitting:
Too lazy to answer
The kid's question.

Farewell to Taoist Scholar Hsu
on his Way to the Imperial Palace

To receive
The Emperor's summons
Alters everyday relationships,
Yet taking no official post
How could you entangle
Your essence?

I know your nature
Is empty as a gourd,
And suspect that zither
Is heavier than you are.
Resting,
Think of nearby clouds;
Walking, wait
For flocks of cranes.

Up in the woods
To bid farewell,
I slowly realize
The simple world.

Delight at a Call by Principal Graduate 'Big' Sun

Tao the same,
We forget 'honored' and 'humble',
And when you're around,
You often visit this rustic lane.

In person
We just use nicknames;
Our poem titles don't note
Official positions.
In our crazy chants
There isn't any malice,
And sitting quietly
Leaves a good feeling.

I'll hate it
When you're back at your office;
The garden and house
Might be hard
To stay around.

White Chrysanthemums

Thick fog? Lots of frost?
Like there isn't any.
A brilliant light
Lights courtyard steps.

Why wait more
For fireflies or snow?
Beside a patch of chrysanthemums
It's fine to read
At night.

Ode to Myself at Forty

Though the idle mind
Remains unmoved,
I realize my memory
Is imperceptibly failing.

Shrinking from go,
It's hard to amuse guests;
When lute-playing comes up,
I call for my kid.
Too lazy to work?
The farm tools believe it.
A scattered person?
My Taoist robes know.

In times ahead
How will I use
Brush and inkstone?
In the shade,
Revising old poems.

Late Autumn Cherishing Thoughts of Master Jun

Wind's pure, Moon white:
The season of red trees.
No cure
For walls of mountain
Between me and Master Jun.

I still love
The deep night,
The creek racing past the steps
Into White Lotus Pond.

Writing the Events of a Summer Day

Normally
I hate going out
The more so in a steaming swelter.

Disinclined
To slip a short smock on,
How can I drag long skirts around?
The pine wind scoffs
At the present of a fan.
And a stone wall's better
Than imperial ice.

Only this poverty
And nothing to do,
Constant melancholy
Not easy to better.

Farewell to the Reverend Wu Yung
Returning to the Chung-t'iao Mountains

Lofty and far
A temple in the Chung-t'iao Range.
Exploring it in autumn
You forget the sheer,
Steep road.

Overlooking a river.
Sandal tracks appear.
Entering the clouds,
A staff's shadow vanishes.
From the Gallery of Statues
You can spot trees in Ch'in.
See Shun's capitol
From a library window.

The spot on the wall
Where I wrote a poem,
Take an idle glance there,
I think you'll start pacing
Back and forth.

Farewell to the Reverend Huai Ku
Going Roaming around Hangchou

Just the day
The leaves fall,
You remember a sky
That bends toward the river.

Gibbons
Sneak across
The roads you travel.
Seagulls
Glide astern
Into the boat.
Loaded
With books of poems,
Your sleeves are heavy.
Bowl and bag
Dangling at the end,
The staff you shoulder
Slants.

Let's set a date
for a temple on West Lake.
We'll look into joining
The White Lotus Order.

PH

～ Wang An-shih (1021-1086)

Selections from Twenty Poems
in the Style of Han Shan and Shih Te

I.

If I were an ox or a horse
I'd rejoice over grass and beans.
If, on the other hand, I were a woman,
I'd be pleased at the sight of men.
But as long as I can be true to myself
I'll always settle for being me.
If taste and distaste keep you upset,
Surely you are being deceived:
Gentlemen, with your heads in the stars,
Don't confuse what you have with what you are!

II.

I have read a million books
Seeking to learn all there is to know,
But the wise always seem to keep it to themselves,
And who would listen to the other fools!
How wonderful, to be one of the Idle Way,
Who leaps clear of each restraining clause,
Who knows that "Truth" lies deep inside the self
And never can come from someplace else.

III.

Puppets are gadgets and nothing more,
None of their kind has roots to tend.
I have been behind their stage
And seen with my own eyes.
Then I discovered the audience,
All their excitement completely controlled,
Fooled by the puppets the livelong day,
Tricked into tossing their wealth away.

IV.

Luck is hard to find when you're down and out,
And easy to lose once you've got it.
Pleasure is what we need after pain,
But pleasure, then, gives birth to greed.
I know neither pleasure nor pain,
I am neither enlightened nor dim.
I am not attached to Future, Past, or Now,
Nor do I try to transcend them.

Allegory

Nothing in the universe can be figured out.
Leaves drop, while pine branches scoff at age.
Still, a blossoming peach makes me feel like a sage —
Here we are, without a doubt, still having doubts!

Miscellaneous Poem

Clouds appear free of care
And carefree drift away.
But the carefree mind is not to be "found" —
To find it, first stop looking around.

On the River

North of the River, autumn's wet umbra
    clears halfway,

But evening clouds, full of rain,
    still remain.

In a tangle of green mountains
    the Way seems to disappear,

Then, all of a sudden, a thousand other sails,
    now there, now here.

JWW

Hui-chu Temple, Mount K'un

Mountaintops emerge and then vanish,
lakes and rivers ebb and flood.

Trees and gardens almost float,
temples and towers swarm across the hill.

A hundred miles of fishing boats,
a thousand hidden homes.

Visitors seldom come.
Bittersweet, sitting zazen with the monks.

SH

～ Pao-chueh Tsu-hsin (1025-▦)

Ninety fragrant days of Spring
the wandering bee delves the flowers.
When all of that fragrance is safe in the hive,
where do the petals fall?

JPS

~ Su Tung-p'o Su Shih, 1037-1101)

Presented to Liu Ching-wen

Lotus withered, no more umbrellas to the rain
A single branch, chrysanthemum stands against the frost
The good sights of the year: remember those
and now too: citrons yellow, tangerines still green.

A Harmony to Ching Hui-shu's Rhymes

Bells and drums from the south bank of the river.
Home? Startled, I wake from the dream.
Clouds drift: so also this world.
One moon: this is my mind's light.
Rain comes as if from an overturned tub.
Poems too, like water spilling.
The two rivers compete to see me off;
In the treetops the slanting line of a bridge.

T'ien-ho Temple

Green tiles, red railings
from a long way off this temple's a delight.
Take the time to take it in,
then you won't need to look back, turning
your head a hundred times.
River's low: rocks jut.
Towers hide in whirling mist.
Don't roar, don't rail
against it. The sound would just fade
in that distance.

Song to the tune nan ko tzu

rapt in wine against the mountain rains
dressed I dozed in evening brightness
and woke to hear the watch drum striking dawn
in dreams I was a butterfly
my joyful body light

I grow old, my talents are used up
but still I plot toward the return
to find a field and take a cottage
where I can laugh at heroes
and pick my way among the muddy puddles
on a lake side path

To the tune of huan chi sha

"I wandered along the Ch'i-shui to Clear
Spring Monastery. The monastery faces Orchid
Creek, and the creek flows to the West."

below the hill the lily shoots
are yet to break the surface of the stream
the sandy path among the pines is dry
though cuckoos cry, in mournful rain
who says that youth will never come again
before the gate the waters still run West
don't let your few white hairs
make you mimic Po's yellow cock
too early crying,
                    morning.

JPS

Drinking with Liu Tzu-yu at Gold Mountain Temple

(I got very drunk, and lay down on Pao Chueh's
meditation platform. Towards midnight I rallied and wrote this on
his wall:)

Bad wine is like bad men,
their assault as fierce as swords and arrows.
Limply ascend the meditation platform
and overcome it by not struggling.
The old poet gets his second wind,
the Zen master's speech pure and gentle.
I'm drunk, almost senseless
aware only of red and green swirls.
When I sober, the moon sinks in the river,
the sound of the wind changed.
Only one altar lamp
the two heroes both out of sight.

CL

Reversible Verse

(Poem read forward)

Inscription For Gold Mountain Temple (I)

Tides follow hidden waves. The snow mountain tilts.
Distant fishing boats are hooking the moonlight.
Bridge facing the temple gate. The pine path is narrow.
Doorsill by the fountain's eye where stone ripples transparently.

Far, far green trees – the river sky is dawning.
Cloudy, cloudy scarlet afterglow. The sea is sun bright.
Viewing the distance: four horizons of clouds joining the water.
Blue peaks are a thousand dots. A few weightless gulls.

(Poem read in reverse)

Inscription For Gold Mountain Temple (II)

Gulls are weightless, a few dots. A thousand peaks are blue.
Water joins the clouds' edges in four distant views.
Bright day. Sea glows with scarlet clouds on clouds.
Dawning sky and river trees are green, and far, far.

Transparent ripples from the stone eye: fountain by the doorsill.
A narrow path and pine gate where the temple faces the bridge.
A bright moon hooks boats. Fishing waters are distant.
A tilted mountain is a snow wave, secretly following tides.

TB & CP

~ Shou Ch'uan (late IIth century)

Returning Alone

under a declining sun, as cicadas cry
I return alone to the temple in the woods
whose rough pine doors are never pulled shut
the slivered moon edging along beside me.

grassy forms crystallize amidst mist-shrouded forces
the scent of blossoms saturates the air with pungent mystery.

now and then I hear dogs barking,
once again press my way between green creepers.

JHS

～ Ts'an Liao Tzu (Tao Ch'ien, c. 1077)

Summer Night

A pine fragrance
Fresh from meditation
Raise
        the curtain
Receive evening's cool
Exquisite, nestled in
        green bamboo,
The moon
Wordless
Crossing the eastern wall.

Morning Awakening

Dark crane trills daybreak
Temple bell stirs the hillside
Clear moon
        slips into the maple grove
Shadows sully my robe.

The Little Hut

One hut holds it all
So where's the sense in great and small?
Precious it is, hermit!
An empty vault without a speck of dust.

Hut Mountain

Tall pines squeeze the road
Sunset bright
Breeze hugs the leaves
Locusts' long, faint drone
Encouraging travelers
to linger a while . . .
Outside the mountains
there is nothing so pure.

Autumn Night on the River

Rain obscures the green river
Evening not yet calm
At the well, phoenix-leaves
stir up autumn's music
Rooftops cut the sigh
of midnight breezes
The moonlight, there, in
floating cloud shallow places bright.

Seventeenth Night of the Eighth Month, Written in a Dream

Midnight
Fall River
No one around
Green lotus lifts from
the dew in fresh flower.
River gods and water sprites
come together to drink.
One handful and I forget
My birth
My life
My spirit

On the Huai River

I.

Reed tips face the dawn
        shivering in the autumn wind
At P'u-k'ou the winter tide
        has not yet come
Sunrise on the sandy bank
        pocked with narrow caves
Pale frogs and dark crabs
        creep without end.

II.

Tonight on the sandy hill
        the moon rises late
Fireflies swarm like rain
        around my boat
Pity their brilliance, though
        it is boundless
Does it match one inch
        of the moon's glow?

III.

Sky broad, dark clouds
        bow and embrace the trees
Sand frozen, terns and egrets
        want human kindness
A small boat anchored . . .
        whose house is that?
With tall bamboo and far off flowers . . .
It seems like Spring.

CL

∾ Chih-tu Chueh (11th-12th Century)

My family lives on Orphan Peak,
all year long, the gate half shut.
I sigh that my body has aged,
but I'll hand on my Way to my children

JPS

❧ K'o Chen (11th-12th century?)

Night in Mid-Autumn

Swift waters; soft, quiet
like gently rustling locusts
I sit in an empty pavilion
alone but for the jagged peaks
the coupled ranges gone white with snow
moonlight has captured the black night

JHS

❧ Shei-an Liao Yen (11th Century)

All that fall's none other than
all that is, not dirt . . .
Mountains, rivers, the great broad earth . . .
or in the dew, is manifest:
Body of the Buddha.

JPS

～ Tao K'ai (d. 1185)

End of the Road

here I am, seventy-six
a life's worth of karma just about gone.
alive, I don't lust for Heaven;
dead, I won't worry about Hell.
I'll loose my grip and lie down beyond the world
given in to fate, freely, without constraint.

JHS

Yuan
1280-1341

～ Ta Kuei (13th Century)

Lone Monk

Under the pines, dark essence
dwells.
One monk sits, or
lies down, alone.
When he's hungry, he'll
find fallen fruit, thirsty,
tip the gourd.

JPS

∿ Po-tzu T'ing (13th-14th century?)

Inscription for a Painting

the withered tree stands tall, craggy
like an old monk.

windblown, rain-bedraggled:
       simpleminded

spring comes; autumn goes, soundless, invisible;
its solitary branches reach up, unbent by the world.

Watching the Flowers

some prefer peach blossoms— swollen, lush;
others the handsome plum-flower, gorged with sap.
my heart too is concentrated on nothing else.

is this allowed?

      and by whom?

JHS

❧ Liao Hsing (d. 1317)

Exhorting Others

a pair of white birds soars into the sky
they never miss the moments of change.
on every side green hills encircle azure waters
straight is the Way, beyond this orb.

Self-Exhortation

I see these hills, hear the streams — and all grief fades
amidst coiled mountains, I cross endless flooded brooks
am lost among steep crags and raging torrents.
timeless and unchanging, each and every twist and turn.

JHS

∿ Ma Chih-yuan (1260-1325)

Evening Bells Near a Temple

Under the thin smoke of winter,
the old temple is quiet.

After sundown,
all the visitors are gone.

On the west wind, three,
four chimes of the evening bell.

How can the old monk
concentrate on zazen?

SH

～ Chang Yang-hao (d. c. 1340)

T'ung Pass

Masses of mountain peaks,
waves as if in a rage —

the road to T'ung Pass
winds among mountains and rivers.

Looking west to the capital,
my heart sinks.

Where the thousand armies
of Ch'in and Han once passed,

I grieve: ten thousand palaces
ground into dust for nothing.

Dynasties rise, people suffer;
dynasties fall, people die.

SH

～ Ch'ing Kung (d. 1352)

End of the Road

the green hills don't ask for bodies and bones
and once you're dead, who needs a grave anyway?
no "flames of Nirvana" for me
my only issue a few sticks of unlit tinder.

Mountain Dwelling

things of the past are already long gone
and things to be, distant beyond imagining.
The Tao is just this moment, these words:
plum blossoms fallen; gardenia just opening.

JHS

Ming
1368-1644

∾ Tai An (d. 1403)

Calling out to Buddha

calling out to Amida is calling your own heart
the heart is Buddha
      no place else.
look to the forests, the pools, the ponds
let day and night sing Dharma's song.

JHS

❧ Miao Hui (15th Century)

Trained Flowers: Wild Grasses

when the mouth smiles,
the heart had better smile too.
where Buddha-nature flourishes,
can dreams be less than rich?

garden flowers and wild grasses are just the same.
others speak out;

      not me.

JHS

～ Tao Yuan (fl. 1404-1425)

Early Plums

ten thousand cold, colorless trees
only their south-facing buds have started to open
trailing faint perfume above the half-thawed current
shadows: closing above my rustic hut.

JHS

❧ Han Shan Te-ch'ing (1546-1623)

Mountain Living: Twenty Poems

I.

down beneath the pines
              a few thatched huts
before my eyes
              everywhere blue mountains
and where the sun and moon
              restless rise and fall
this old white cloud
              idly comes and goes

II.

when plum petals among the snows
              first spring free
from the ends of night
              a dark fragrance flies
to the cold lantern
              where I sit alone
and suddenly storms
              my nostrils wide

III.

through a few splinters of
              white cloud motionless
the Buddha wheel bright moon
              comes flying
to accompany me
              in my mountain stillness

and I smile up at it
    above the dirty suffering world

IV.

it only took a single flake
    to freeze my mind in the snowy night
a few clangs to smash my dreams
    among the frosted bells
and the stove's night fire fragrance
    too is melted away
yet at my window the moon
    climbs a solitary peak

V.

through a face full of clear frostiness
    raw cold bites
through a head overstuffed with white hair
    a gale whistles
and over the world from flowers of emptiness
    shadows fall
but from my eyes the spells of darkness
    have completely melted

VI.

in the sh sh murmur of the spring
    I hear
moon clear the primal Buddha pulse
    come from the West
with motionless tongue
    eternally speak
how can I be sad again?
    how strange

VII.

in the dark valley the
        orchid scent is overwhelming
and at midnight the moon's form
        so gracefully sways by
like a sudden flick of the
                stag tail whisk
reasonless it
        smashes my meditation

VIII.

in its Buddha flash I'd forgot all
        reason quieted in contemplation
when an orphan brilliance glared on
        my meditation, startling me
and I saw off through the void
        lightning strike
but it wasn't the same
        as that firefly beneath my eyes

IX.

clouds scatter the length of the sky
        rain passes over
the snow melts in the chill valley
                as Spring is born
and though I feel my body's like
        the rushing water
I know my mind's not
        as clear as the ice

X.

I'm so rotted out

I should pity these weak bones
but look! my consciousness is reborn
            my mind strengthens
day and night my back
            is like an iron rod
constant and pervasive is my meditation
            like an evening's frost

                XI.

in the empty valley
            all filth is wiped away
but this bit of lazy cloud
            stays on
for company I have the pine branches'
            twitching stag tail whisks
which is almost enough deer
            to make a herd

                XII.

words
            an enchanted film across the eyes
ch'an
            floating dust on the mind
yet all ins and outs become one
            with one twirl of the lotus
and the chilocosm
            whole in my body

                XIII.
a quiet night
            but the bell toll will not stop
and on my stone bed dreams and thoughts
                alike seem unreal
opening my eyes

I don't know where I am
until the pine wind sounds
                    fill my ears

                    XIV.

like some pure clarity
                    distilled out of a jeweled mirror
the Spring waters
          fill the many lakes
reflect up into my eyes
          here on Mt. Lu
and the moon above my forehead
          becomes a bright pearl

                    XV.

six on the lotus clock?
          the stick's too short
and on the incense piece
          where's the century mark?
day and night are truly constant
          and stop nowhere
to know immortality in the morning
          hold in your hand the womb of the flower to be

                    XVI.

though a slice of cloud
          seals the valley mouth
a thousand peaks
                    scratch open its emptiness
and in the middle
          are a few thatched huts
where hidden deep is
                    this white haired mountain man

XVII.

what a pity the blue mountains
                go on forever
this old white hair is petrified
                of the time to come
and plans to burn himself out
                amongst the inns down in the dust
anyway who ever heard
                of a lazy transcendental?

XVIII.

on the mountainside
                mournfully sipping the night rain
to the pine sounds
                throat choking on clear frost
gone to beg food
                this Buddha's priest is a tired bird
until the moth brow crescent
                moon arises new made up

XIX.

the world shines
                like a watery moon
my body and mind
                glisten like porcelain
though I see the ice melt
                the torrents descend
I will not know
                the flowers of Spring

XX.

outside my door
                blue mountains bouquet

before the window
       yellow leaves rustle
I sit in meditation
       without the least word
and look back to see
       my illusions completely gone

JMC

❧ Ta Hsiang (d. 1636)

Poet's Zen

no hiding the pain I feel as twilight darkens
incense from India may not be ritual enough.
every day, after chanting the Heart three times,
I give in, again, to the seductions of poet's Zen.

JHS

Ch'ing
1644-1908
&
Republican Era
1911-present

❧ Shih Shu (c. 1703)

the human body is a little universe
its chill tears, so much windblown sleet
beneath our skins, mountains bulge, brooks flow,
within our chests lurk lost cities, hidden tribes.

 wisdom quarters itself in our tiny hearts.
liver and gall peer out, scrutinize a thousand miles.
follow the path back to its source, or else be
a house vacant save for swallows in the eaves.

. . . .

as flowing waters disappear into the mist
we lose all track of their passage.
every heart is its own Buddha;
to become a saint, do nothing.

enlightenment: the world is a mote of dust,
you can look right through heaven's round mirror
slip past all form, all shape
and sit side by side with nothing, save Tao.

JHS

❧ Yuan Mei (1716-1798)

Rolling up the Curtain

Rolled up the curtain on the window, North,
wind blows, Spring's colors, cold.
One monk, one sprig of cloud,
together at Green Mountain's peak.

Monk's Place

Monk's place
                    I
lean the painted rail.

Eyes play
                    gazing
on the plain.

A little rain
                    beyond
a thousand miles.

An evening's sun
                    reds
half the village.

Breeze cool,
                    a sense of flowers
gathering.

The hall is small
                    the Buddha's incense
mild.

There, where, last night
                    we played
at chess . . .

On mossy step
                    a fallen man
lies still.

Late Gazing (Looking for an Omen as the Sun Goes)

I

Window's dark, roll back the curtain's waves:
what's to be done about sunsets?
Climb up and stand, in some high place,
lusting, for a little more last light.

II

From a thousand houses' cook fires' fumes,
the Changes weave a single roll of silk.
Whose house, the fire still unlit, so late?
Old crow knows whose, and why.

III

Golden tiles crowd, row on row:
men call this place the Filial Tombs.
Across that vastness, let eyes wander:
grand pagoda: one wind-flickering flame.

By Accident

Here, I've seen every temple,
asking naught, as the Buddha knows.

But the moon came
                          as if to rendezvous,
and the clouds went off
                          without goodbyes.

In the inns a decent bite to eat
                          was hard to come by,
But in my carriage
                          poems came easy.

Going back the baggage will be heavier:

Two or three seedlings of pine.

Late, Walking Alone to a Temple in the Mountain's Cleft

Four sides green peaks

wind, make a wall.

Though the eaves drip rain,

in the hall, there's sunlight.

Look hard, but can't make out

the way I came.

I turn, and ask the monk

how he got here to greet me.

Temple of the Bamboo Grove

Late, passed the Temple of the Bamboo Grove.
In slanting sun, the corners of the walls
sunk deep in shade.
Windy lamp, the red unsteady.
Misty willows, green, held deep and still.
Monks few, stone chimes are often silent:
trees many, sunlight, and shade too.
Ears catch a hint of Buddhist chanting:
my horse's bells have a pure clear tone.

Just Done

A month alone behind closed doors
forgotten books, remembered, clear again.
Poems come, like water to the pool
Welling,
                    up and out,
from perfect silence.

Gone Again to Gaze on the Cascade

A whole life without speaking,
                    "a thunderous silence"
that was Wei-ma's Way.
And here is a place where no monk can preach.
I understand now what T'ao Ch'ien, enlightened,
said, he couldn't say.
It's so clear, here, this water
                    my teacher.

P'u-t'o Temple

A temple, hidden, treasured
                    in the mountain's cleft
Pines, bamboo
              such a subtle flavor:
The ancient Buddha sits there, wordless
The welling source speaks for him.

Mornings Arise

Mornings arise
to find ten thousand kinds
of pleasures.

Evenings sleep: the single
mantra (now, the heart) is
nothingness

No knowing in this world
which, of these ten thousand things, is
me.

Motto

When I meet a monk

        I do bow politely.

When I see a Buddha

        I don't.

If I bow to a Buddha

        the Buddha won't know,

But I honor a monk:

        he's apparently
        here now.

Just Done

Possessed of but a dwelling place
the heart may rest in quiet.
The flavor of disirelessness
lasts longest.
So a boy runs off
to snatch at
        floating willow silks:
If he didn't capture them
        how could he let them go?

Mad Words

To learn to be without desire
        you must desire that.
Better to do as you please:
        sing idleness.
Floating clouds, and water idly running —
        Where's their source?
In all the vastness of the sea and sky,
you'll never find it.

Nearing Hao-pa
*(I saw in the mist a little village of a few tilled roofs
and joyfully admired it.)*

There's a stream, and there's bamboo,
there's mulberry and hemp.
Mist-hid, clouded hamlet,
a mild, tranquil place.
Just a few tilled acres.
Just a few tiled roofs.
How many lives would I
have to live, to get
that simple.

Laughing at Myself for Lazing Around at West Lake
(having started the year with poems planning to go
to T'ien-t'ai with Liu Chih-ping)

It takes a lot of bamboo strips to make a little sail,
it only took a few to make these sandals.
But to get from sailing on West Lake
to walking up T'ien T'ai mountain . . .
You could say that in my thousand mile trek to find a Zen Master
I stopped off first down in the country, to gab with my good old
friends.

JPS

∾ Hsu Ku (19th Century)

Poem of Thanks

while my body's at home, my heart takes a little trip
right or wrong, good or bad, who can tell?
the only valuable thing in life is enlightenment
a tree full of blossoms: a sliver of sunset clouds.

JHS

～ Ch'an Ch'eng (19th century?)

Before My Eyes

The fragrance comes in
at the window: a light breeze,
sun not yet setting.
Awake, after I slept
through the midday session: Spring,
a pair of swallows drop in
take a sip from the flower.

JPS

~ Ching An (1841-1921)

Night Sitting

The hermit doesn't sleep at night:
 in love with the blue of the vacant moon.
The cool of the breeze
that rustles the trees
rustles him too.

Written on the Painting "Cold River Snow"

Dropped a hook, east of Plankbridge.
Now snow weighs down his straw rain gear.
It's freezing.
The River's so cold the water's stopped running:
fish nibble the shadows of plum blossoms.

Returning Clouds

Misty trees hide in crinkled hills' blue green.
The man of the Way's stayed long
at this cottage in the bamboo grove.
White clouds too know the flavor
of this mountain life;
they haven't waited for the Vesper Bell
to come on home again.

Over King Yu Mountain With a Friend

Sun sets, bell sounds, the mist.
Headwind on the road: the going hard.
Evening sun at Cold Mountain.
Horses tread men's shadows.

On a Painting

A pine or two,
three or four bamboo,
the hut on the cliff is quiet.
Only the clouds come to visit.

Moored at Maple Bridge

Frost white across the river
waters reaching toward the sky.
All I'd hoped for's lost
in Autumn's darkening.
 I cannot sleep, a man
adrift, a thousand miles
alone, among the reed flowers;
but the moonlight fills the boat.

Crossing the Yang-chia Bridge Once More

The face reflected in the stream's
 lost half its youthful color.
Spring wind
is as it was before,
so too, the thousand willow boughs.
Crows perch to punctuate
the lines of slanting sunset.
It's hard to write
as I pass this place once more.

At Hu-k'ou, Mourning for Kao Po-tzu

Though he was young, Kao
was the crown of Su-chou and Hu-k'ou.
It was only to see if he was still here
that I came today to this place . . .
found a chaos of mountains
no word
this evening sun
this loneliness.

Laughing at Myself

Cold cliff
withered tree
this knobby pated monk . . .
thinks there's nothing better than a poem.
Laughs at himself for striving so
to write in the dust of the world,
and scolds old Ts'ang K'o
for inventing writing,
and leading so many astray.

JPS

~ Po Ching (Su Man-shu, 1884-1918)

The sea, the sky
where dragons were, I go
to war.
Blood in a bowl is water, black, mysterious,
and earth, yellow.

Hair wild, song long and
steady, as you gaze out
on the ocean's vastness.

Yi Shui, The River of Changes, sighing
soughing, when the ancient Ch'ing K'o
set out toward a hero's death:

Now, then, one sky, one
moon, all white,
an emptiness as pure
as frost.

Written at White Cloud Ch'an Hall Beside West Lake

Where white clouds are deep
Thunder Peak lies hidden.
A few chill-plums, a sprinkle of red rain.
After the fast
oh so slowly
the mud in my mind settled out.
The image in the pool before the hut:
                        fallen from that far off bell.

Passing Pine Bank, I Was Moved

Orphan lamp drew out
 a dream, a memory
a moonlit and shadowy confusion
then wind, and rain.
From the next door hut the
midnight bell.
When I came again, you'd gone.
All that crossing of rivers, that
plucking hibiscus, for whom?

Passing Rushfields

Where the willow shade is deep
the water chestnut flourishes.
Endless, silver sands
where the tide's retreated.
Thatched booths with wine flags flapping:
know, there's a market near.
A whole mountain of red leaves:
a girl child carries kindling.

Passing the Birthplace of Cheng Ch'eng-kung
Last Loyal Defender of the Ming

A passer-by points far off, and says,
"That's Lord Cheng's Rock."
White sand, green pines, beside the setting sun
As far as you can see
how many sons of China left?
Monk's robe, and tears
bow down
before the memorial stone.

To Mei-wen in Kuangchou

Just now: heart flagged to hear
the neighbor's girl so sweetly singing,
and I thought
what's that "Southern Poet" up to now?
So I wrote a couple of lines
just to ask news of you.

Here the flowers fall like rain:
so much sadness in all this chaos.

Having Hope, or Holding On

In this life, to become a Buddha
How could I hope . . .
Hermit dreams are undependable
and my desires unconquered.
Many thanks, my friend
for all your kind inquiries,
but I suspect my fate's
to be just a poet-monk.

From Japan

Spring rain on the pagoda roof,
and the shakuhachi's sound.
Will I ever see the Chekiang tidal bore again?
Grass sandals, broken bowl, and no one knows . . .
Treading on the cherry blossoms I will trudge
across yet one more bridge.

Headed East, Goodbye to an Elder Brother

Rivertown's a picture
run from our overturned cups.
Together just a moment, this time:
how many times harder to part?
From here the lone boat, the night,
bright moon.
Parting the clouds, who'll gaze out
upon the tower.

JPS

~ Hsu Yun (1840-1958)

Sound of the Wind in the Pines
an Afternoon and Night on Mount Lu

I.

Courtyard-covering white dew
Moistens hidden orchids.
Leaves fade; a few flowers
Half retain their scent.
The cold Moon hangs alone;
Nothing happening with people.
Pine wind blows right through:
Night waves cold.

II.

Swell after swell of pinewind
Comb like waves at sea:
Beat after beat of heavenly music
Strummed on cloudy strings.
Midnight, Tao folk
Purify their hearing
And rise alone to burn incense:
Moon full
Just overhead.

III.

Zen heart peaceful and still
Inside white clouds.
Autumn floods and spring mountains

Aren't the same yet.
It's just the pine wind
Whistles another tune.
Deep night white moon,
Drizzling already.

IV.

The mountain is empty; flute still.
Thought uninvolved.
A pine wind circling the cabin
Calls right through the ear.
Here's a monk with a talking habit;
Midnight, the eternal teaching
Preaching 'No Birth.'

Written for the Zen Man Te-jun at the Great Assembly at Fo-yen

Days long ago do you remember
Making circuits of the Buddha halls?
How could we know the age of Earth,
The Boundless steppes of Heaven?
Chariots of wind I have ridden
And caught tigers on cloud-sprung feet.
Undersea I snared a dragon,
Moonlight streaming through the window.

Outside of time, flowers of wonder bloom,
Stamens touching space.
At sky's edge moon trees
Breathe laurel perfume.
Again I walk the pure, cool, earth;
Form-taking life thrives in the web,
Upholding the Dharma-king.

At a Thatched Hut on the Flower Peak of Mount T'ien-t'ai
Sitting with Dharma Master Jung Ching During a Long Rain

Hard rain, our gathered firewood scant;
Lamp frozen, glimmers not at night.
In the cave, wind blows stones and mud.
Moss engravings weatherstrip rickety door.

Brooks in torrent untiring;
People's words more and more rare.
Where schemes calm heart?
Sitting in the lotus,
Wrapped in robes of Zen.

Feelings on Remembering the Day
I First Produced the Mind

Drawn some sixty years ago by karma
I turned life upside down
And climbed straight on to lofty summits.
Between my eyes a hanging sword,
The Triple World is pure.
Empty-handed, I hold a hoe, clearing a galaxy.

As the 'Ocean of Knowing-mind' dries up,
Pearls shine forth by themselves;
Space smashed to dust, a moon hangs independent.
I threw my net through Heaven,
Caught the dragon and the phoenix;
Alone I walk through the cosmos,
Connecting the past and its people.

PH

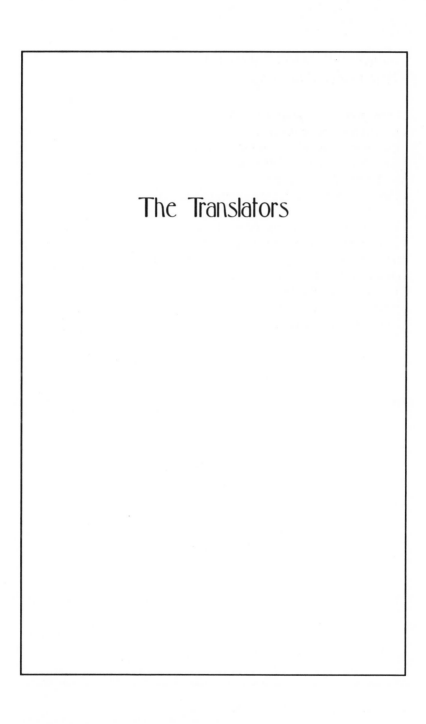

The Translators

TONY BARNSTONE has published many translations of Chinese poetry in literary magazines and is the co-author of *Laughing Lost in the Mountains, Selected Poems of Wang Wei* (Wesleyan University Press). His most recent book, *Out of the Howling Storm,* also from Wesleyan, is an anthology of contemporary Chinese poetry.

RICHARD B. CLARK, translator of the *Hsin hsin ming,* or verses on the faith-mind, by Seng Tsan, is resident teacher at the Living Dharma Center in Amherst, Massachusetts.

JAMES M. CRYER, winner of a translator's grant from the National Endowment for the Arts, is the author of *Plum Blossoms,* the complete poems of China's greatest woman poet, Li Ch'ing-chao, and translator of the poems of Li Po in *Bright Moon/Perching Bird* (Wesleyan University Press). He is presently completing a book of translations by Po Chu-yi.

SAM HAMILL's translations from Chinese include *Banished Immortal: Visions of Li T'ai-po, Facing the Snow: Visions of Tu Fu, The Art of Writing* (by Lu Chi)< *Endless River,* and *Midnight Flute.* He has also published two dozen other books including translations from Japanese, ancient Greek, Latin, and Estonian, and ten volumes of original poetry and essays. He is Founding Editor at Copper Canyon Press.

PAUL HANSEN, also an NEA grant winner, makes his living as a painter and printmaker. Hansen's poems have appeared in numerous literary magazines. Among his books are *The Nine Monks* and *Lin He-jing: Recluse-Poet from Orphan Mountain* from Brooding Heron Press and *Before Ten Thousand Parks* from Copper Canyon Press.

CHRIS LAUGHRUN is presently studying Chinese at the University of California, Berkeley.

JOSEPH LISOWSKI is presently Professor of English at the University of the Virgin Islands. His poems and translations have appeared in numerous magazines, including *Negative Capability* and *The Literary Review.* A selection of the poems of Wang Wei, *The Brushwood Gate,* was published in 1984 by Black Buzzard Press.

CHOU PING, who is presented here as co-translator with Tony Barnstone, is a contemporary Chinese poet who writes mainly in English. His poetry has appeared in many literary magazines, and a large selection is featured in the anthology *Out of the Howling Storm*.

JAMES H. SANFORD is the author of *Zen-Man Ikkyu* and editor of the acclaimed volume of essays on Buddhist esthetics *Flowing Traces* (Princeton University Press). His recently co-authored (with J. P. Seaton) translation of the complete poems of Shih Te, with harmony poems by Ch'u Shih and Shih Shu, *Shadowed Pines and Twisted Boulders,* will be published by Broken Moon Press. He teaches Asian religions at the University of North Carolina.

JEROME P. SEATON, professor of Chinese at the University of North Carolina, Chapel Hill, has authored and co-authored several books of Chinese poetry in translation, including *Wine of Endless Life* (White Pine Press), *Bright Moon/Perching Bird* (Wesleyan University Press) and *Love and Time* (Copper Canyon Press). He is an advisory editor of *The Literary Review*.

ARTHUR TOBIAS is the translator of the poems of Han-shan in White Pine Press' *The View from Cold Mountain*.

JAN W. WALLS is presently completing a book of translations of the poetry of Wang An-shih. His translations have previously appeared in *Sunflower Splendor* and *The Literary Review*. He is the director of the David Lam Centre for International Communications of Simon Fraser University in Vancouver.

Suggested Reading

Robert Aitken, *Taking the Path of Zen,* North Point Press, San Francisco, 1982.

Robert Aitken, *The Mind of Clover,* North Point Press, San Francisco, 1984.

Robert E. Buswell, Jr., *The Zen Monastic Experience,* Princeton University Press, Princeton, 1992.

Heinrich Duoulin, *Zen Buddhism: A History,* 2 Vols., MacMillan, New York, 1990.

Jan Fontein and Money L. Hickman, *Zen Painting and Calligraphy,* Boston Museum of Fine Arts, Boston, 1970.

Thich Nhat Hanh, *Being Peace,* Parallax Press, Berkeley, 1988.

Thich Nhat Hanh, *Call Me By My True Names: The Collected Poems,* Parallax Press, Berkeley, 1993.

Jack Kornfield, *A Path With Heart,* Bantam Books, New York, 1993.

Kenneth Kraft, ed., *Zen Tradition and Transition,* Grove Press, New York, 1988.

David Pollack, *Zen Poems of the Five Mountains,* Scholars Press, Decatur, Georgia, 1985.

Bill Porter, *Road to Heaven: Encounters with Chinese Hermits,* Mercury House, San Francisco, 1992.

Red Pine, *The Zen Teaching of Bodhidharma,* North Point Press, 1987.

Gary Snyder, *Riprap and Cold Mountain Poems,* Grey Fox Press, San

Francisco, 1958.

D. T. Suzuki, *Zen and Japanese Culture,* Princeton University Press, Princeton, 1973.

Shunryu Suzuki, *Zen Mind, Beginner's Mind,* Weatherhill, New York, 1970.

Burton Watson, trans., *The Zen Teaching of Master Lin-ch'i,* Shambala, Boston, 1993.

Alan W. Watts, *The Way of Zen,* Vintage Books, New York, 1957.